BARE SOUL

BARE SOUL

Poetry

Kalpna Singh-Chitnis

PARTRIDGE
A Penguin Random House Company

ISBN: Softcover   978-1-4828-5055-0
             eBook   978-1-4828-5056-7

The Library of Congress has cataloged "Bare Soul" as follows
Author and Copyright Claimant - Kalpana Singh-Chitins
Also known as Kalpna Singh-Chitnis
Registration Number - TX 7-674-707.
Registration Date, February 5th 2013

Print information available on the last page.

To order additional copies of this book, contact
Partridge India
000 800 10062 62
orders.india@partridgepublishing.com

www.partridgepublishing.com/india

Contents

Dedicated to the Great Masters!

Acknowledgment

I'm grateful to Jennifer Reeser, John Harricharan, Jack Foley, Amata Natasha Goldie, Satyapal Anand, Michael Burch, Robbi Nester, Athina Merkouris, Akhtar Islam and Farah Siddiqui for their suggestions and support.

I also want to acknowledge *California Quarterly, Levure littéraire, World Poetry, Poetic Diversity, The Enchanting Verses, Tower Journal* and *Life and Legends* in which several poems from *Bare Soul* first appeared.

My special thanks to my children Shashwat, Vishwa and Nirvan, who are the first readers of my poems, and everyone else who has inspired and supported the publication of *Bare Soul*.

~ *Kalpna Singh-Chitnis*

Dear Kalpana!

I am really Thank feel
for your Outlook towards life and love
This world needs beautiful Souls like yours

yours *Amrita*

अमृता प्रीतम

Amrita Pritam - Janapith Award, Sahitya Academy Award, Vaptsarov Award and Officier Ordre des Arts et des Lettres award winner Punjabi Poetess and Author, India.

"*Bare Soul.* Whose soul? Ever since *Leaves of Grass* first appeared in 1855, we find Walt Whitman simultaneously falsely imitated and truly manifesting in America. Who would have thought that his latest local incarnation would be in the body and the soul of an exceptional woman born in Gaya, Bihar, India, where the Buddha experienced Enlightenment? Yet here he is..." ~ *Jack Foley.*

Introduction to a Major Poet
Kalpna Singh-Chitnis' "Bare Soul"

It is clear, and here at last – the first collection in English from one of India's most revered and gifted living poets, Kalpna Singh-Chitnis. A "First Lady" of Hindi letters, before the age of twenty-one years, Kalpna had already received the prestigious "Bihar Rajbhasha Award". Following her "crowning" with a second title, that of "Bihar Shri", (which translates to "The Jewel of Bihar"), Kalpna continued to garner praise from notables such as Nobel Prize nominee Dr. Wazir Agha (who wrote the introduction to "Nishant," "The Dawn," Kalpna's third collection). Academy Award-winning lyricist Gulzar penned the preface to "The Investigation Continues," her second collection – which also, incidentally, contained an introduction penned by Kedarnath Singh, who holds the highest literary honor bestowed in India. She has been endorsed by other icons of the Eastern Hemisphere. Legendary figures of Punjabi, Urdu and Hindi literature such as Punjabi poetess Amrita Pritam wrote of her from Kalpna's earliest years as a published poet. The tradition continues to this day, as one may see by the remarks in praise from Sir Naseer Ahmed Nasir, a man with double nominations for this year's Nobel Prize in literature. As though these things were not enough to recommend Kalpna's writings to the Western, English - speaking world, she also holds "Rajiv Gandhi Global Excellence Award" in both film and literature – a private award given in New Delhi, an event attended by the Indian Head of State, cabinet members, celebrities and foreign dignitaries in recognition of significant achievement in various disciplines on both national and international levels.

These things have taken place on the sub-continent of India. But Kalpna has lived half her life in the United States, and it is here and now, with the publication of this collection, that she establishes herself as a poet of the West, and the English tongue, as well. Indeed, her verse may remind the reader of Rumi, the Sufis and mystics – but Rumi, the Sufis and mystics in fine English, with an ear for its native rhythms. Her lines bear only a vague reminiscence, "echoing" these masters as one might repeat the details of a dream upon awakening. For Kalpna's voice is as original and cross-cultural as it is universal and classic. She dedicates this collection to the great masters, and with credibility, as her genius crosses borders.

"In one poem, for example, she might be speaking with English poet Percy Bysshe Shelley, through her use of the nightingale – invoking with timeless relevance Shelley's metaphor from "A Defence of Poetry," where Shelley observed that the poet is a nightingale who sings in solitude, comforting the self through song."

Or look at movement two of "Ancient Remorse," a poem in which the speaker questions Jesus, or movement three of "On a Good Grey Day," both of which the reader could imagine to be lyrical "reincarnations" of passages from English poet Christina Rossetti, sharing complex themes of renunciation, desire, and spiritual supplication, while also holding in common an innocence of expression, and uncomplicated speech. These are poems in which the poet's voice assumes the sanctity of a Buddhist or Christian nun with equal believability. Her use of the crown of thorns, crosses, her allusions to the messianic and "faith like a child," her empathy with the savior, her angels and demons, a sacred chalice, her deep themes of self-sacrifice for the sake of love and the redemption of a soul, thanksgiving and praise for the eternal – all these will be well felt and comprehended by the Western heart and mind.

But just as we are finishing, turning the page from the voice of this "nun," the poet varies that voice in "Devil's Dilemma," placing a demon's mask before her like some unforgettable Japanese Kabuki player, delving into the dark depths of human nature. But despite the seeming evil of such a persona, all the while, this "holistic" poetry heals. Because if we believe what psychologists and many students of the soul tell us, that the first step toward healing is to recognize and confess our condition, then this poetry can be called "vital", in the sense of that word which means alive and life-giving. In some lines, the poet gives this life almost through a series of "shock treatments," with surprising, dry humor, with startling, disturbing images such as those of scorpions crawling inside the human heart, lava oozing from it, and whispering serpents; or "Ancient Remorse, VII" where the speaker becomes a sort of New Age Juliet, a metaphorical suicide, swallowing poison in order that her love may become immortal...

Above all, this is a book of love. Major poets seldom introduce any new truths. They simply re-state those things we know to be true, expressed in their own individual ways. From the poet's opening verses, where the jungle is used as a microcosm for humanity, Kalpna urges us to maintain our unique identities, whatever those identities may be, reinforcing in her own way Shakespeare's wisdom, "To thine own self be true." And while human nature is never exalted over the divine (in fact, one overwhelming theme is the longing for union with the divine), these are poems which always call us back to our common, core human values. These are the verses not only of a major poet, but of a true humanitarian. In an era when core human values no longer seem common, Kalpna writes again and again with insistence about the priority of love, in all the forms it takes. Although it is quiet and submissive, never commanding, never phrased so imperiously or emphatically, hers is a philosophy which harmonizes well with Auden: "We must love one another or die." No, this poet only cries, "I can't afford not to love anymore!" From section I of the aptly-titled, "Ancient Love," where the Beloved is an erotic obsession, to section V where the poet speaks in total, devoted submission to the Creator through images which are nearly lurid, to section VI, where a parent sits up all through the night with a child.

It is my privilege to introduce this major poet, this Jewel of the East, to a new hemisphere, and the New World.

Jennifer Reeser

Critically-acclaimed author of *"An Alabaster Flask,"* and *"Sonnets from the Dark Lady,"* and the bestselling epic, *"The Lalaurie Horror".*

June 2014

Introduction

Every once in a while, I sit back and reflect on the vicissitudes of life and living, the mysteries and meanings of what we encounter in this long and strange journey on Earth. And in reflecting, I get lost in my thoughts about the various feelings experienced by those who are traveling this road.

Yes, but that's not the whole story. I also look for those who could share with me and with others, their thoughts, their experiences and their feelings about their discoveries along the way. There are many who do so, but they do it with such "dryness" and "ordinariness" that the true messages are lost among the noise of their minds.

Imagine how delightful it would be to really meet someone whose essence radiates deep, heartfelt feelings of joy, wisdom, pain, sorrow, ecstasy and all the facets of the human experience. And how beautiful it could be to have that "someone" share with you his or her perspective and understanding with such deep integrity, honesty and child-like simplicity that sometimes, you weep bitter tears, or you roll on the grass with uncontrollable laughter and amusement. Yes, only a poet could touch your soul that way.

But you may wonder if such souls exist. I can assure you that they do because, not too long ago, or, perhaps longer than I may ever recall, I bumped into just such a personality who expresses thoughts with feelings, ideas with joy, power with peace and complexity with simplicity. That person, among her other talents, writes and recites poetry that speaks to the heart of the reader or listener. In her collection of poems called, "Bare Soul," Kalpna Singh-Chitnis brings to you the story of yourself and your relationship with your world.

Only a poet of Kalpna's caliber could make words sing and dance or weep and mourn all at the same time. Kalpna, in her collection of verses brings to you her "Bare Soul," which you soon discover is not only her story but, the story of you, the reader.

As you read or listen to her poems, you will find yourself standing beside her by the seashore, the wind blowing gently through your hair and the voices of seagulls making loud but comforting sounds in the distance. You may find yourself walking with her through a dry, hot desert land only to come upon an oasis with cool, pure water and a large comfortable tent.

Or, you may find yourself transported to magical places where, perhaps, you partake in mystical adventures as you listen to sweet music and subtle love songs in the evening breeze. Such is the power of the poet! Such is the gift of the poet! All this and more, you will find in the poems of Kalpna in her volume called, "Bare Soul."

Thank you, Kalpna, thank you for sharing such deep parts of your heart and soul with all of us. Once your words have touched us, we can never be the same again. We will become more tolerant, more understanding, not only of others but, of our very selves. May you keep on writing and sharing with us.

John Harricharan, award-winning author of *"When You Can Walk on Water, Take the Boat"* and other bestsellers.

Foreword

I feel honored to be invited by Kalpna to write the foreword for her fourth poetry book. "Bare Soul" is a collection of her greatest poetic works which will stand the test of time in the purity of her offerings.

Poets seek to know the language of the soul. We desire to experience the many varied landscapes of the soul's journey, to drink in the nectar of life and to write of the human experience.

~ It is this that the poet craves:

The vibrancy of the inner life,

The exploration of the soul,

We seek to dive to the depths,

And soar to the heights

We want to taste the kaleidoscope

Of Life's banquet ~

It is with this understanding I explore Kalpna's writings. I have been fortunate to have shared a divine poet friendship with Kalpna over the years, each of us understanding the depth at which the other is writing from. It is this connection that is like the breath of life for a poet. To express from deep within, to feel and be felt, to move your readers, to plunge to the depths and then to uplift, is also why a poet is compelled to put words upon a page.

Kalpna bares all in her book "Bare Soul". This poetry collection is undoubtedly the language of the soul. Kalpna writes with heart and soul, her essence, poured out onto a page, is untouched by any other force. She writes with the presence of ancient poets such as Rumi, Hafiz and Omar Khayyám.

Her soul is ancient and yet her incarnation is contemporary. Her poetry transcends the boundaries of literary analysis, soaring above the need to categorize or dissect or label with names as much of English literature is approached. There is no need to discuss her use of metaphor, of rhyme, of alliteration or allegory. These poems are not pre-meditated, re-worked or painstakingly constructed. They are the arrows which shoot forth in purity from the depth of Kalpna's soul.

It is this immediacy of delivery in which her presence is felt instantaneously. The reader is drawn into the radiant riches of the heart; both compellingly and urgently. It is this transparency, this raw truth of being who Kalpna is in her totality, that draws a gasp from our souls, as we recognize our own true self, reflected in her mirror.

Her words point to the potential we all have to be real, daring, courageous and utterly transparent. It is this blazing authenticity that hides no-thing. When we read a poem by Kalpna, it is our true self that is engaged. The potency of her presence removes our masks. We are invited upon a spiritual pilgrimage into the heart of ourselves. It is only a fearless soul that can lead us there. Kalpna is Buddha's Warrior, and we, as the willing reader, must be brave enough to fall under her magical poetic spell.

Kalpna's poems paint masterpieces through the exploration of universal themes. The themes expressed deeply in her work are: Love, Union, Joy and Sorrow, Time,

Transcendence, Life's' Journey, Immortality, Light and Dark, Longing, Duality, Divinity, Self-Knowledge, Impermanence and the Eternal.

The collection of poetry in each sub-section reveals timeless themes. My impressions I have shared with you as they may shine the light for the reader seeking to gain another interpretation of the poems, outside of one's own. Reading a poem will touch something different within us all as we all have unique insights and we will all be moved in different ways.

The body of work of 'Ancient Love' embodies a breathtaking love and a poignant sadness. These magical poems speak of an ancient mystery; they dance beyond the world of form and duality into the eternal. Deeply revealing and personal, these poems are for all the lovers dotted across the world.

The poems encompassed within 'Ancient Quest' explore the theme of union; of the eternal longing to unite. They pierce into the heart of Loves' sacred quest and speak of an intangible desire. This desire is a universal desire that vibrates upon many levels of the human experience. These poems reach to us to follow our souls calling and realize our inherent potential. This is beautiful poetry that can sweep one's heart away into the cosmos and beyond.

This body of work within 'Ancient Remorse' speaks from a universal presence, from the One that is all-pervading. The theme is a mystical union with our Creator, and the beauty of universal love. These poems show compassion for our spirit being encapsulated within a mortal existence.

In 'Being Nothing and Everything' Kalpna explores the divinity of ourselves in everything. These poems speak of the jewel of self-knowledge.

We meet with our inner child in 'Conversations with a Friend'. These poems show a boldness and directness and convey a peaceful defiance. They have profound meaning and depth and are symbolic of the polarities of life. These works ask the eternal questions and the reader must listen for the resounding answers. It speaks of a never-ending quest and whispers of self-realization.

Within 'Devil's Dilemma' we are shown the beauty of light and dark. Kalpna gives us instant darts of insight and shared awakenings, often shocking the reader with her startling ending lines that capture the totality of the poem.

'Firebird' is one of my personal favorites; its presence illustrates great mystical poetry. I see it as a reflection of the poet's soul that is forever unconquered. Of a life that is an unending quest.

The collection of poems within 'On a Good Grey Day', show the human experience of dark nights and 'grey days' of the soul. These poems are a call to awaken and are a reminder to be fully present in the Now moment. They speak of the impermanence of life and the relentless passage of time. Kalpna invites us to experience a pure revelation of Self, guiding our awareness to the totality of existence. Here she shows a deep soul awareness embodying a connection with All That Is.

The poems within 'Rain' depict our connection with the elemental. They speak of the deliverance of the soul and the return to our Creator. These poems are symbolic of our divinity and examine the strength of the human spirit. The reader is encouraged to enter into self-enquiry and seek our own transformation.

Within 'Rustling Winds' we voyage beyond form into the formless. We are shown the essence of the mystery of being and given life's lessons. Kalpna uses poetic imagery to show us the beauty of the soul and its innumerable experiences.

The poems contained within the set, 'Touched by the Devil', reveal a kaleidoscope of emotions and illustrate human vulnerability. The poet questions the dark self in an exploration of heaven and hell metaphors, touching also upon the theme of rebirth. These works show the strength of the human spirit despite the dark night of the soul experience. Kalpna takes us upon a journey into the unknown and leads us ultimately to a revival of our soul.

In 'Unkind', we are shown the truth of our inseparable connection with each other. These little poetic gems portray pain and ecstasy through the themes of dream and reality.

Kalpna's life reads as an unending quest. Her poetry is great mystical poetry. Her words are a reflection of a soul that is unconquerable. Read 'Bare Soul' and surrender your own soul to the pure magic of Kalpna.

Amata Natasha Goldie, Poet and Author of the "*The Golden Thread Book.*"

JUNGLE

I

The jungle greets century a new year,
centuries greet millenniums;

millenniums greet eternity,
and eternity greets the sacredness in us.

Let's rise in gratitude,
and blossom like wild flowers;

open to the core,
and perfume the jungle!

JUNGLE

II

Let's bare ourselves,
and bask in the beauty of the jungle.

Let's throw away our covers,
we've had enough of them!

In the jungle there is no need to pretend,
let's just be, whoever we are.

Let's be the lions, eagles, wolves, hyenas,
deer, doves, deities or serpents; if that's what we are...

Or let's be the trees, hills, rocks, dunes
or fallen leaves on a winding trail.

Let's celebrate our thirst
searching for a stream;

let's glow in our skin
in the darkness and light;

let's dazzle,
when the sun plays hide and seek;

let's bare our souls,
and keep the sacredness of the jungle;

let's discover now,
our wild inner beauty!

JUNGLE

III

The jungle has caves,
but no cages.

It has a freedom unchained,
for everyone.

The jungle has no rules but one,
to have no rules, but disciplines.

The jungle has one language,
only to be heard in the silences,

and its meaning to be discovered
in the outburst of our joy!

JUNGLE

IV

Every birth in the jungle is a celebration,
there is no death in the jungle
ever to be ever mourned.

The jungle breathes life in all deceased,
in the jungle
everyone resurrects,

every tear is counted,
and becomes an offering
to the river of eternity!

RIVER OF SONGS

I

I opened my eyes
and found poetry before me.

I turned my back on it
to face reality,

ever since I'm transformed into
a river of songs!

RIVER OF SONGS

II

A river takes all
good or bad;

the heart of a river
does not discriminate;

everything becomes pure
as the river flows...

RIVER OF SONGS

III

Who claims to know
what the river is all about?

Those who came in their boats of pride,
could barely make it to the shore.

Those who came without any prejudice,
could never surface to tell its depth.

Who claims to know the river?
Not the river itself...

RIVER OF SONGS

IV

Truth is not always what is said;
truth is not always what is heard;

sometimes, the truth exists somewhere in the middle,
and flows with the course of life like a Silent River;

committed to the world on both its sides,
searching for its way to the ocean.

ANCIENT QUEST

I

It's now time for me to empty my soul,
roll into the abundance of silences,
to hear my voice...

It's now time for me to pour myself
into the chalices of some restless hearts,
and let my intoxication be the exhilaration of others...

It's now time for me to become one, with the vastness of the ocean,
and let all the waves come crashing,
to shatter my pride...

It's now time for me to light the candles, and let myself be a firefly,
entering the periphery of your light,
and become immortal...

It's now time for me to wear the charms you gave me once,
feel the warmth of your invisible embrace,
and let my heart thaw...

It's now time for me to be, what I haven't been before,
sip the night in ecstasy,
from your sacred tranquil lips...

It's now time for me again, to write nights in your name,
and be afraid to lose,
to my stars once again...

It's now time for me to hear, the heart of the ocean,
throbbing in a seashell, washed off the shore,
a heart very similar to yours...!

ANCIENT QUEST

II

After a long journey
I have found you.

Now resting at your threshold
in this moonlit night,

I'm waiting for you to know
that I'm here.

I have come all the way
not to try your love for me;

I'm here to tell –
I can't afford not to love anymore!

ANCIENT QUEST

III

There is a happiness you can't share;
there are sorrows you can't express;

reaching to a dead end proves to be an illusion,
when it comes to life and love.

Welcome to the humble abode of my soul,
that longs to hear your footfalls,

and hold you in my arms,
for eternity...!

ANCIENT QUEST

IV

Good or Bad,
I can't discriminate!

Right or Wrong,
I'm not aware of it!

Seeing you before my eyes,
I turn into a waterfall,

You are my ancient thirst!

Seeing you no more,
I leap into the darkness for light,

You are my ancient quest!

ANCIENT QUEST

V

There is a nook in my place;
nobody walks in there but me.

One night, when the moon was pale,
and my heart mute, I saw you there...

I never told you where I live,
how did you find out?

Or do you think, it wasn't you?
That it was just my dream resurrected?

ANCIENT QUEST

VI

When I try to reach you,
you step back;

when I try to let go,
you follow me everywhere...

I don't know,

whether you are my obsession,
or I'm yours?

ANCIENT QUEST

VII

I wear you like my soul,
and become full of life.

I dwell in your thoughts,
and feel loved.

Our distance strengthens
my ability to endure.

Your invisible touch
perpetuates in my pores.

Why should I search for you elsewhere?
My joy, you are always within me!

ANCIENT LOVE

I

Something that feels right
when all your six senses are awakened
that's your truth,
and you are one of them.

A gift from the heavens, wrapped in my breath,
that I unfold every day,
with much joy and gratitude.

I worship the ground
where we stood,
and saw the incarnation of our ancient love.

Children wonder,
what do I hear in the winds, that they can't hear?
What do I see in your being, that they can't see?

For them, you are my obsession;
for me, my journey
and an island in the ocean of mysteries,
never lost from my sight.

ANCIENT LOVE

II

Broken into atoms,
I fervently search for you;
my body is no longer my limitation.

Your existence pulls me like a cosmic magnet,
and I have no clue, should you ever ask me,
why am I like this, the way that I am?

I'm nothing but an explosion in space and time,
my self is no longer mine,
and I seem to have no control over anything,

but I know one thing for sure:
I can't be a disaster
for nothing!

ANCIENT LOVE

III

When I try to close my doors at you
I break into a million pieces.

When I try not to hear my voice
you become louder than a thousand prayers.

When I try to lose your sight
I drown in a hundred rivers.

When I try to escape your thoughts
I'm captivated in your invisible arms.

So here I am once again before you
without any resistance!

ANCIENT LOVE

IV

Buried in the dust of time
my eternal bliss
you have quivered on my lips once again,

and rolled into my eyes
like a storm
never occurred before.

After a long time
I have felt blossoms in my pores
and spring in the air for me to breathe once.

In a long time
silences have found their meanings
not spoken in words,

but only to be written
with our hands
on the forehead of time.

ANCIENT LOVE

V

Paint me gold like the sunshine;
color my eyes river-green;

color my tresses with the color sapphire;
color vermilion my lips;

paint the moon as a dot on my forehead;
and eyelids sparkle with stars;

paint my hands with the hue of the henna;
and borders of my feet with morning rouge;

color my days with the colors of the rainbow;
color my nights with the color of your light;

color my heart with the color of yours;
color my love just simply pure;

paint me, O painter! As the world awaits,
for the finest creation of yours!

ANCIENT LOVE

VI

All night,
it rained silently;
it is as if,
the sky unburdened its heart.

All night,
you held my hand by my bedside,
and I slept like a baby
all night.

All night,
the sun, moon and stars
prayed for me
in their very hearts.

All night,
I was the most blessed child.

ANCIENT LOVE

VII

The fragile ground we stand on is stone cold,
and in the darkness, as we unchain each other
from our hurt and remorse,
the lava of centuries oozes from our hearts,
and we float into each other's eyes.

We savor the darkness bestowed upon us,
leading us toward each other,
our wings are bruised,
and there is no sky above our heads,
but we have what the heavens don't;

like a twine in the candle,
we burn together, we light together!

ANCIENT REMORSE

I

I gave myself away,
and my crown, treasure,
empire and swords
were all yours at once!

The only thing I had left was
my childlike faith in you...

Then what was that doubt
in your mind my warrior,
that you had to shackle me
and walk me through the crowd?

To prove your valor,
was there really any need
of a crown of thorns for me?

ANCIENT REMORSE

II

"Kindness", the most fascinating word for me
and "Love" so mysterious,
so I went to Jesus and asked
to interpret their meanings for me.

"Ethics", the most misinterpreted word
and "Trust" the most invaded,
so I went to Jesus and asked
to restore their meanings for me.

"Hope", the most wanted word by all,
but some prayers not answered at all,
so I went to Jesus and asked
to explain their reasons for me.

"Love" and "Faith"
two most humiliated words in the dictionary of life,
so I went to Jesus and asked
to glorify their meanings for me.

Jesus looked at me and smiled,
a teardrop trickled down his eyes,
and I could not ask him for anything, anymore,
but I had my answers for sure!

ANCIENT REMORSE

III

My thoughts are void of words;
like a tide on a full moon
crashing by the shore,
I return to myself...!

My mind is void of thoughts;
like a night without light,
reaching unreachable,
I surprise myself...!

The winds are void of life;
like an unmarked grave,
with my destiny to wait,
I identify myself...!

My thirst is void of mortality;
like a wanderer in the desert,
searching for the rain,
I mystify myself...!

The sky is void of horizons;
like a nightingale in the darkness,
singing to the moon,
I renounce myself....!

ANCIENT REMORSE

IV

I shall echo in you,
become a void.

I shall dance with you,
be the music.

I shall sparkle in you,
be the light.

I'll make sense to you,
be reasonable.

I'll mean a world,
be no one.

I'm always here,
if you do not pretend,

without any beginning,
without any end.

ANCIENT REMORSE

V

Rooted in defilement,
my heart like a pond of
fresh lilies!

In my silences,
I hear the serpents whisper;
in my pure intoxication,
I let the scorpions crawl
right into my heart!

In my fearlessness,
I do not refuse anything,
that you have to offer me
in the name of love and trust,
assurance and appreciation;

neither do I resist my tears
as you unveil,
you have given me the glory of tasting
the sweetest venom of life
that I accept,

challenging my every impending death,
promising a new life every time
with my last breath.

ANCIENT REMORSE

VI

You come to fill me up to the brim,
so that even if I breathe,
all will fall from the cups of my eyes,
that I have been hiding from you.

River of love, untamed by times
when floods,
only drowns
skillful swimmers like me...!

ANCIENT REMORSE

VII

Let it go,
let it go...
I tell myself submerged under the water.

From my faint breathing bubbles form,
and shatter before my eyes;
and my tears swell up the ocean,
as you drag me down
deeper and deeper...

Let it go,
let it go...
I say it again,
and let your hand go
from the grip of my hand...

You float away from me,
disappearing in the womb of the ocean,
right before my eyes,
and I cry letting you go
like losing a child...

Let it go,
let it go...
I whisper again and faint,

now unable to enter the womb of my mother again...!

ANCIENT REMORSE

VIII

Down under the moon,
I embrace the earth,
on a cold winter night,
my heart must feel the frost,

and my lips must burn,
as I swallow the venom
to make my love immortal.

The moon is no longer the same,
as it was gifted to me by you,
and I wonder,
how to fathom the depth of your skies,
where I lost my precious stars?

Escaping the black holes of fears,
I try to reach you in your dark heavens,
seeking mutual salvation,
not scared of the past, not scared of the future,
my love so fearless, my love so pure,
like a river of light...
breathing the moments,
walking on the milky way.

Love isn't an audacity,
it's simply brave, I reason,
as the skies come crumbling down,
and my poem for you takes its last breath in my hands...

Have you seen a love so short lived?
Have you seen a love still so proud?

ANCIENT REMORSE

IX

Straining out the fallen stars
I drink from the cup of the moon,

your promises never fulfilled,
his grace forever unending.

IN THE VESSEL OF KNOWINGNESS

I

In the vessel of knowingness,
voices echo,
my heart sinks,
and I try to hold tight,
to my breathing...

my mind unable to grasp all
helplessly looks for a clue,
someone needs to keep me awake,
for me to put the rest
to sleep.

IN THE VESSEL OF KNOWINGNESS

II

I see the vessel breaking
and myself swimming across
the vast emptiness;

going beyond the extremes of
knowing and not knowing,
happening and not happening,
being and not being;

looking for a place
existent and non-existent,
searching for my joy
eternal and annihilated.

RUSTLING WINDS

I

You gave me nothing;
I had nothing to take care of,
nothing to worry about;
you set me free from everything.

You took everything away from me,
and became my prisoner for the lifetime.

RUSTLING WINDS

II

Every time when it has been plundered
my wealth has become double;

take my treasures away once again
if needed,

without any disguise
great masters!

RUSTLING WINDS

III

You want me to free you from guilt,
but I'm neither the lock, nor the key;
both are in your hands my friend,
set yourself free!

RUSTLING WINDS

IV

I'm not worried about
where you go every night,
I'm just sad to see you empty handed
when you return every morning!

RUSTLING WINDS

V

I won't question,
where you go
when you are bewildered,

what you do,
who you spend your night with
I'm neither a beloved, nor a wife,

I'm simply your home!

My roof is to give the shade you need,
and my walls to keep you warm and safe,
without ever questioning your return.

My windows are to bring air and sunshine,
and my door to welcome
every time you return;

and like no other,
my heart like a wind chime to greet you
in the rustling winds;

and like prayers, I travel in the air
when you set out to the destinations
known and unknown;

only to ensure your safe return home,
every time,
when you are lost!

RAIN

I

Sad like a monsoon sky,
weepy like pouring rain;
aimless like rolling clouds,
silent like vast plains.

Rain,
come down,
extinguish me, I'm inflamed!

Shiver me like a twig breaking from a tree,
shatter me like a drop fallen from the roof,
bring me down,
I'm nothing but a mud house!

Rain,
rush me through the raging rivers,
for me to lose all
what hurts and can't be cured!

Rain,
come down,
and be the angel of my salvation!

RAIN

II

Rain,
pour on me
till I'm swept away from the ground,

crushed by the mountains,
flushed by the streams,
and lost in the roots of the jungle!

Rain,
I must give all,
what it takes me to be me,
what it takes us to be us,
without having each other...!

RAIN

III

Rain,
I won't go seeking a roof,
I need nothing over my head;
drench me in your purity,
make me vulnerable,
soak me to perfection,
so that one can see through my robe,
a soul, bare naked behind all!

Rain,
continue to fall,
I have survived all,
I will survive all!

RAIN

IV

Rain,
help me unearth the mystery,
I want to see, how far the roots of this tree go,
that blossoms my love even after its fall?

Rain,
take me to its life-source,
help me wreck the centuries, millenniums,

help me find the day -
when the seeds of miracle were sown
transforming my heart into a garden...

Rain,
I'm turning cold and pale,
help me unveil,

to return to the warmth
and comfort of mother earth.

FIREBIRD

Firebird,

stretch your wings and fly high,
under the blazing sun
into the saffron skies...!

Fly across the deserts without any oasis,
searching for a caravan
without any footprint...!

Fly across the oceans of tears and hurts,
without any island
enlivening your thirst...!

Fly over the mountains
without trees or nests
or any final place for you to ever rest...!

Firebird,

light the sparks in the fallen stars,
siphon the volcanoes
hidden in our hearts..!

Firebird,

come on down and take a rest,
before setting out on
an unending quest...!

Rescue the songs from the rising flames,
and walk barefoot
on the fire again...!

Conquer the skies,
forever unconquered,
and ask the questions that have never been answered...!

Firebird,

fly to the lands of the glorious remains,
on your undefeated wings
bring down the rain...!

TOUCHED BY THE DEVIL

I

I'm a timeless enchantress,
with many faces,
hungry and deceitful.

I plunder the hearts of the impoverished,
enslave them
and look innocent.

I belittle the angels,
and coax the devils;

I dare to touch the flames,
and blame it on the fire;

I jump off the cliffs,
and blame it on the mountains;

I point finger,
and wage wars!

I reside under a cool pond
like an ugly, slimy frog,
pretending to be a lotus.

Are you kidding,

I can't be real, if I cry desert,
and be thoughtful to give the rain
to the thirsty souls like mine.

I can't be real,
if I claim to love in a way,
no one has loved before!

I'm the biggest farce,
I must be laughed and stoned,
and I must not expect anymore.

Not even the Messiah should come near me,
and I must endure all,
without showing any hurt, any remorse!

It's my fault,
if I didn't tell,
who I am;

ice or the fire,
earth or the wind,
pauper or a queen!

How dare, I wore you like my soul,
and went out to tell the universe,
that I was happier and warmer than the heavens?

I shouldn't play games,
and if I do, my nerve must be questioned,
and I must be tried in the heavens,

I must be stripped off my soul,
and my body must be hung in the sky,
stapled onto the blue moon,

so that the world can see,
and learn from my example.

Yes, I must remain Unforgiven,
for all my sins,
at all times...!

TOUCHED BY THE DEVIL

II

Feeling like a brick-wall,
you can hit your head on it,
not advised though!

Break me down,
bring me earthquakes,
reduce me to dust,
I shall recreate myself.

This time,
I shall sprout from the womb of a seed
hidden in me,
that you can't see.

This time,
I will survive
without any rain, wind or sunshine.

This time,
I will exist beyond all,
as I have existed before;

before the birth of the sun, moon and stars;
before the formation of rain, winds and storms!

This time, I will exist in a timeless tranquility,
far, very far away from you...!

TOUCHED BY THE DEVIL

III

Angels in the heaven warned me,
do not play with the fire,
fire isn't for a naive breeze
wanting to brave the ocean.

I looked at the angels, smiled,
bowed to them, and offered my heart
to the live flames!

The Devil rose from the fire at once,
held my hand and whispered -

"Your heart is the last thing
I shall ever ask from you.
Take it back..."

He gave me my heart back,
and walked away in disbelief!

My heart,
now unable to reclaim its place
I wear on my sleeves,
that I can give it to you, or you,
if you ever ask for it.

But, it isn't about giving,
it's about accepting,

a heart humbled by the angels,
touched by the devils,
tested by fire!

TOUCHED BY THE DEVIL

IV

Invaders descend from the heavens like angels
and I give all,
but they don't stop coming,
I often have restless nights.

Looking at the stars behind the tall trees,
I sleep in the wreck of the day,
and something falls from my eyes,
shattering on the floor, like marbles.

I get up, and feel tempted to walk
on the broken pieces...
I want to dance, in solemn darkness,
to the tune of an unbearable pain.

My heart beats,
and my feet bleed
as I begin...

Weighing the sky all night
with my arms up,
whom do I summon?
What do I desire?

I don't know...
I don't want to know!

DEVIL'S DILEMMA

I

The Devil said,
don't hold me precious!

The pearls, about to fall from your eyes,
make you the wealthiest in the world!

Now, don't give me the temptation
to look into your eyes again!

I can't steal anything from you anymore,
and can't heal your bruised wings.

I belong to the world where you can't soar,
and I can't fly!

(Poetry in paradox)

DEVIL'S DILEMMA

II

Angel,

I can't stop to read the prayers
you write for me on the dunes everyday.

I have very little time left to cross the desert,
in search of a beloved
I have been looking forever.

(Poetry in paradox)

DEVIL'S DILEMMA

III

Angel,

I'm thirsty for the wine that tastes likes yours,
from the cup my beloved pours...

I want to feel the warmth of your wings,
under the spell my beloved casts...

I want the freedom of your soul,
in the arms my beloved wraps around...

and I have returned to you, only to learn,
if there is any way to make these things possible,

without any prayers...?

(Poetry in paradox)

DEVIL'S DILEMMA

IV

Angel,

I can't open my eyes to the sunshine,
do not open the door...

I'm unable to understand the enigma of life,
do not speak simplicity...

I won't be able to reveal,
no need to heal...

accept my apology
and leave...!

(Poetry in paradox)

DEVIL'S DILEMMA

V

Angel,

I don't understand,
why you sing for me when I can't hear?

Why you watch over me,
when I'm lost in slumber?

Why you don't think twice,
before being alone with me, day and night?

Aren't you afraid of turning into a devil yourself?

The angel stopped singing for a moment,
and asked the devil -

"What is Self?"

(Poetry in paradox)

DEVIL'S DILEMMA

VI

I tell every angel - I'm a Devil,
but they don't believe me;

they take me home,
give me food, wine and love.

They give me honor, I don't deserve;
they give me trust I can't keep.

I'm a Devil,
I must do things my own way!

(Poetry in paradox)

UNKIND

I

When it wants to rain from my eyes,
I know there has been a drought in your heart!

It shall rain again,
so that you can grow all what you need;

and like an empty cloud, I shall drift away
at your one unkind gesture.

Poets will write songs about me
and the world shall sing.

No worries,
if you are out of words with me

once again...!

UNKIND

II

You may throw rocks,
and wait for the ripples to form,

but you are no longer a child,
and I'm no longer a pond!

UNKIND

III

Your hands try to reach me
and I hold them close to my heart,
like the hands of a child
frozen cold in winter!

I do not question,
what you would do
with the warmth of my body and soul,
when you shall depart;

or when you are baffled and confused,
at the break of dawn
on what to call me,
a dream, or a reality?

Unlike you,
I do not question!

BEING NOTHING AND EVERYTHING

It has been bruised
trampled and abandoned,
but it won't die.
It's my ego!

I never said I'm a Buddha,
and the day I shall become one,
would I be here to tell
who I am?

Angels of my salvation,
I'm just a human,
and I must be honest about who I am,
a sheep in a lion's clothing,
or a lion with all my pride!

If I'm fire
I must ignite.

If I'm wind
I must blow in the direction my heart indicates.

If I'm rain
I must pour out to quench thirst of millions like me.

If I'm sky,
I must stretch my wings and fly...

To be Nothing, I must be "All"
and to be All, I must be "Nothing" at last!

A PALE MONDAY MORNING

I

I went to sleep late last night,
and woke up early this morning.
A very kind note to a friend
wasn't kind enough!

I woke up feeling sad and knowing
that sometimes we unknowingly
touch the hearts of others,
only to create ripples.

Sometimes,
ripples aren't bad,
yet, it's okay to feel sad,
only to understand the heart of a pond,

filled with sadness.

A PALE MONDAY MORNING

II

The Christmas sun is not warm enough,
and there is no fireplace in my house.

I stand alone in my patio,
hoping for some sun flakes at noon,

knitting a warm winter hug
with my tangled breath,

for a recipient unknown!

A PALE MONDAY MORNING

III

How do you deal with your sadness?

I just made a cup of tea and forgot to drink it,
watching the pollen falling from the pepper tree!

There is no God to pray to, and no angels to sing,
nothing to hold on to, nothing to set it free...

I just watched the pollen falling from the pepper tree,
turning me yellow and scented, like the earth...!

CONVERSATIONS WITH A FRIEND

I

A little girl inside me
does not want to grow up.
She wants to go with you
and conquer the world.

The little girl inside me comes,
sits on these steps every day,
and lets her heart melt in the sun
while awaiting you.

The little girl makes the sky wonder,
what will happen,
the day she grows up
and stops believing in miracles?

CONVERSATIONS WITH A FRIEND

II

What difference does it make,
whether you can look into my eyes or not,
when I'm sunken into your pores like the daylight,

and the earth you lie in self-defeat
despite all your valor,
borrows my heart to throb inside you?

Friend,
what I can never hear from you
is explained on your silent lips, engulfing my soul.

But no expectations at all, as I never had,
as I always had a way of going beyond all,
what was not meant for me.

And regardless of my defiance,
how can I deny -

you are my undying celebration
without gratification;

an unending quest
without destination;

an endless freedom
without emancipation;

and hidden in you
is a self-realization.

CONVERSATIONS WITH A FRIEND

III

If I'm not here,
I'm there with you.

When you look outside,
I'm inside you.

When I'm not speaking,
I'm listening to you.

When I'm no longer a search,
I'm in a realization with you.

When the ripples in the pond subside,
I'm in the reflection with you!

CONVERSATIONS WITH A FRIEND

IV

I'm a silence after your celebrations,
a melody in the air without expectations;

a missing face in your happy crowd,
a wish that you can't say out loud;

a spot still tender in your heart,
like a meaning hidden in an abstract art;

I'm a humble grip on your restless mind,
the day when choices aren't kind;

I'm a rebel soul in your utmost captivation,
a calm amidst all your tribulations;

a question among all your answers,
and an answer among all your questions;

I'm a shade in the sun in your days of isolation,
an obscure island, in your deepest emotions;

I'm a silent splash in the river of time,
a note of love on a fateful shrine!

I'm a drop in the heart of an endless ocean,
eternal amidst all realizations;

I'm all but me, if you could really see,
but not the one you want me to be;

I'm a choice of your destiny you can't undo,
I know my friend, what am I to you!

COMING HOME

I

Homecoming princess
kind and considerate,
beautiful and true,
be ready for your coronation now,
the time has come!

Hold the bouquet
and smile for the cheering crowd,
don't be surprised,
You were destined to be
who you are today!

Come home,
a warm welcome awaits you,
and a feast of a lifetime,
with kith and kin.

Homecoming princess
bask in your glory,
join the celebrations,
and make a wish.

Homecoming princess
blow out the candles,
burning now
for so long!

And one day,
the homecoming princess
truly returns home,
after a long time!

She gently knocks at the door,
but the walls crumbled,
doors collapsed,
windows evaporated,
and her garden turned into
a handful of dry leaves.

Night owls scattering dust,
came from nowhere,
screeching in broad daylight,
vanishing into thin air...
a fairy tale ends,
not to be told, ever again!

COMING HOME

II

Tangled up in a spider web
I hold back my tears,
standing in a rubble,
still wanting to call it home!

I see eight, bright shiny eyes
looking straight at me,
hanging upside down,

and from the distance of a thousand miles,
my little boy shouts -
"Black widow,
mama, watch out!"

But, I was destined to be bitten...

Not very many people will ever know,
I'm poisoned now!

COMING HOME

III

I slept in the rubble of a home
that was no longer mine,

hoping no one sees me there.
What an embarrassment I have become!

I slept in a cot on the terrace,
pretending to be a little girl,

lying in the moonlit night,
gazing at the stars in summer skies,

long before my poet was born!

I stayed awake all night,
only to hear the voices
I very much wanted to hear again,
but no one spoke!

Not even the spirits,
who supposedly lived in our house, not to hurt anyone,
making me wonder -
where the hurt comes from after all?

I thought of the womb that gave me birth,
and the hands that held me tight,
when I learned,
how to walk the earth.

But here,
I'm all alone.
No one to share a laughter,
no one to partake of my pains!

I looked in every corner,
invaded by the shadows,
and thought of my grandma -
looking for her in the stars,

hoping she would tell me a story
I could believe in it again.
A child must not stop believing
in fables, at no cost!

ON A GOOD GREY DAY

I

Life like a book opened will close,
before we come to know its end.

Eyes filled with dreams,
will turn into ashes someday,
by a riverbed...

and with the winds
we shall fly again,
in the forests, deserts and skies...

we will go back there again,
to where we have come from.

Like everyday,
the sun will rise again,
and come near my window,
looking for me...

I do not know,
who will dare to dream
of embracing the sun that day,
and die for it...?

Or maybe the sun will not come out
of the gloom?

I also don't know,
what will happen to my last song,
left at my desk that day...?

ON A GOOD GREY DAY

II

In the moments of my solitude,
I sit in front of my desk
and think about life.

I think about life and its debts,
I think about its credits and dues,
I close my eyes and write,
I do not need a light.

I still do prefer darkness in abundance
on a good grey day.

What is left anyway,
in keeping an account of some bygone days,
and the nights passing by?

I decide to leave everything at once,
and go somewhere...

I rise and see,
the rain pouring on my glass window,
and a flood outside...

Now out in the torrent,
I'm waiting for some aging walls to fall inside my heart;

I would like to make a paper boat again,
with the remaining chapters of my life...!

ON A GOOD GREY DAY

III

I'm not saddened by the thoughts of coming with you now.
All I want is to give away everything that I have,
before going.

Let me give away all my jewels;
the pearls I always loved,
and the diamonds I never desired.

Let me give away my songs,
abandoned in the book of romance,
and the assurances that I could never give to myself.

Let me free all the rainbow birds of my dreams,
and shed the last remorse
from my burdened heart.

Let me look one more time through my window,
where I sat all these years, and it is as if,
waited only for you to come.

Yet, let me leave my door open;
in case someone comes
looking for me,
long after I'm gone...!

FOURTH MOMENT

I went into slumber and woke up in a new body;
I took my first step and stumbled upon rocks;
and my journey to sufferings began once again.

I sat silently for years,
trying to remember, what was it,
that had the ability to heal?

But now I can't recall...
I can't remember those profound words,
that once comforted my heart and mind,
and those belongings, that supported my body...

I ran year after year, without stopping,
searching for the things,
often looking for my own footprints
in the dust of time,
only to lose myself, all over again...

I summoned heavens and earth to erupt,
to help me find my precious jewels,
lost in the upheavals of Samsara...

I'll recognize them in a flash,
if I ever find them again
as I'm able to see myself in a moment,
beyond past, present and future,
walking my way,

blessed by the great masters,
once again!

BARE SOUL

Who am I?

With the sparks of the shooting stars in the skies,
and fire of erupting volcanoes in my heart?

Storms of the deserts resound in my mind,
dark rolling clouds thunder in my soul.

The speed of the winds determines my pace,
I ask for the rain, for the touch of its grace...

Am I fire
or wind?

Am I clouds
or rain?

Am I stars
or space?

Or a bare soul
without any face?

Impressions

Bare Soul. Whose soul? Ever since *Leaves of Grass* first appeared in 1855, we find Walt Whitman simultaneously falsely imitated and truly manifesting in America. Who would have thought that his latest local incarnation would be in the body and the soul of an exceptional woman born in Gaya, Bihar, India, where the Buddha experienced Enlightenment? Yet here he is: "It's now time for me to empty my soul, / roll into the abundance of silences, / to hear my voice." Kalpna Singh-Chitnis's Bare Soul is a rapturous Song of Herself erupting in a time/space she calls "the jungle." Her always accessible words touch deep chords of emotion in readers looking for something more than intellectual play. Sensual longing has always been at its most intense when it crosses over into mysticism, as it does here again and again. "I can't be a disaster for nothing," she says: "Paint me gold, like the sunshine, /color my eyes river-green." Singh-Chitnis is a filmmaker as well as a poet, and she knows that films give us access to things we cannot touch—"things" like (in the case of Bertolucci's *The Last Emperor*) "The Forbidden City of China." Words/poetry give us access to *other* "forbidden" areas—areas resonant with spirit and its sustaining influence. It's all here in *Bare Soul*: "let's discover now, / our wild inner beauty."

Jack Foley, Poet, Critic, Author of *Visions & Affiliations: California Poetry from 1940 to 2005 and EYES: Selected Poems* – (USA).

Kalpna Singh-Chitnis's poetry is ladened with original thoughts, spontaneity of expression and sublimity. One can feel and peep through her soul by reading her poems, and can easily conclude her knowing of the purity of a soul and belief, that a soul is not a disguiser, and the body is merely a costume.

Her poetic myth and philosophy are self-created and universal to the core. She depicts spirituality in her simple structured poems, as simplicity itself breeds spirituality. Like every good poet nostalgia is one of the peculiar features of her poetry, thus making it like surrendering of self to an ancient dream, flowing through a bygone era and remembering a forgotten love.

She writes with the truthfulness of emotions influenced by an intuitive whiz, creative piquancy and true pre-requisites of poetry from her inner self. Her poetry is like mystic figures drawn on fogged window panes with fingers, that readers, whilst reading enter into a never ending world of perception and touch of feelings. After reading Kalpna's poetry, it is apparent that her creative being will keep on gaining immortality from the fire of herself, nurturing her creativity like the Phoenix.

I believe that Kalpna's poetry is not a nine days' wonder, because her poetic quest is towards an ultimate infinity.

Naseer Ahmed Nasir, *Poet and* Author of "*A Man Outside History*" *(Pakistan).*

Kalpna's engagement is with life. In her poetry, she displays a deep understanding that our journey in this world is riddled with challenges, which causes great sufferings. She writes in a state of Zen and deep contemplation. She is patient with herself, as she tries to process her thoughts, emotions and events of life.

Through the medium of poetry, she looks at life, human bondages, fragility and contradictions. She convincingly delivers a message in a subtle manner. Her poetry flows like a river, which instinctively knows, when to change its course, and flow, when it must.

A painter expresses on canvas with brush strokes, Kalpna does that in the words that immediately draw the reader's attention, as her choices of themes have universal appeal. She, bares her soul, and shares its struggles and evolution with poignant loving kindness towards herself. She seems to have internalized the teachings of Lord Buddha. Suffering is inevitable; one has to look deeply to develop understanding, insight and compassion.

Having lived across the continents, she draws her metaphors and symbols from the country of her origin to where she has travelled and settled in. Her language has no ambiguity; thoughts flow with great clarity, and sometimes with amazing serenity. I feel herein lies the strength and appeal of her work. I have no doubt it will withstand the test of time.

Mamta Agarwal, Poet and Writer - (India)

"Bare Soul" by Poet and Filmmaker Kalpna Singh Chitnis is an extraordinary work of art. Such magnificent image flow in words. Her literary creation and experiences transports you into a great world of emotions. It is fabulously molded by simplicity with such devotion to life and love.

This wonderful soulful poetry sparkles like the poet herself, expressing a profound intensity of feelings, empathy and wisdom. Kalpna's poems enchant through her being, to explode like fire in depth, leaving you wanting more of her insight to bathe your soul.

Capture the experienced journey of sufferings melted with love in the mature verses of wisdom in clarity straight from the heart. I highly recommend this limitless gem "Bare Soul". It will transfer you to the world of the sweet favorable unknown in abundance.

Ghadeer Soudani, Author of *"Clinch the Moon"* and other original love poems – (USA)

Kalpna is a name of six letters, opening the seventh aspects of nature. Her poetry reflects the invisible truth and gives a new meaning to it.

Eternal love is ancient and quest for it is unending. Whatever color you add to it, it will retain its uniqueness. Kalpna's poetry gives special color to its own quest.

To me, Kalpna's poetry emerges from the huge waves of the ocean, after which a reader chases to trace the voice of an unspoken song that surrounds the universe.

Khursheed Hayat, Urdu Writer and Poet - (India)

"Bare Soul" by Kalpna Singh-Chitnis is by far the most extraordinary dramatic love poetry collection I've ever read. The title itself captivated me and stirred my imaginations. Once I started to read the book, I got totally spellbound, struck with awe and overwhelmed with deep feelings.

For me, a woman's love is a mystery. But as Tennessee Williams said, "Some mystery should be left in the revelation of character..., just as a great deal of mystery is always left in the revelation of character in life, even in one's own character to himself."

A series of entitled poems in this book appears to be a confession, and a daring-do for a woman.

Tamara Galiulina, Poet and Photographer (Russia)

Kalpna's poems are like an elixir of love to comfort the longing heart. The allure of colorful imagery sweeps through the core to dance on the canvas of artistic creation without fear and takes the poems to a new height. The passionate embrace of worldly wisdom and sophistication melts the ice into liquid magic.

Bare Soul is an illustration of self discovery, and a treasure trove of creative expression. I'm in awe and admiration of these poems from a place that is so deep and where fear does not exist.

Athina Mekouris, Poet and Fashion Designer (Australia)

Bare Soul: A Commentary

For a lexicographer 'you' is the nominative and objective form of address for the second person pronoun, and no more. For a poet it has multiple meanings. It could be a direct address to anyone in an internal monologue including one of the many personae of the poet. As an address, better known as 'dramatic monologue', it presupposes the second person.

These poems, though divided into various parts, are all sequential. In the first sequence of Kalpna's poems, 'you' is always at the receiving end, collecting, as it were, all her contentious complaints or irenic and self-effacing admissions. Sometimes the speaker is belligerent. At other times it is just a grumble noise bordering on a jeremiad, but it is always there, in a person qua person situation. Let's try to find out from her verse itself who this anonymous 'you' is. Let us take a visualized scenario. It is raining outside, and...

"All night,
it rained silently;
it is as if,
the sky unburdened its heart.

All night,
you held my hand by my bedside,
and I slept like a baby
all night.

All night,
the sun, moon and stars
prayed for me
in their very hearts.

All night,
I was the most blessed child."

A caregiver, an affectionate lover, is reminded of a certain night when, holding her hand, he prayed on his knees by the bedside where the protagonist, a 'beloved' slept 'like a baby'. A couple of other examples we will also take.

"There is a nook in my place,
nobody walks in there but me.

One night, when the moon was pale,
and my heart mute, I saw you there...

I never told you where I live,
how did you find out?

Or do you think, it wasn't you?
That it was just my dream resurrected?"

The 'lover' is now presented as the only other presence in the otherwise secluded 'nook in my place', a deep furrow inside the hidden self, where no one is allowed. If he knew he was there doesn't matter to her. All that was important was the fact that she knew he was there. The eastern influence in terms of the other self in a Mithun incarnation or a Yang Yen avatar is evident in all poems in this section.

It is the second segment that gives to the readers more than they can absorb. It is no longer a meek female part of Mithun that articulates herself; it is assertive. Partnership, yes; submission, no, that's the Summum-Bonum of all short pieces in this section. The lines quoted below from two different poems do not mollify; they might even ruffle the feathers of the male part of this God-ordained union.

"I gave myself away,
and my crown, treasure,
empire and swords
were all yours, at once!

The only thing left, I had was,
my childlike faith in you...

Then what was that doubt
in your mind my warrior,
that you had to shackle me
and walk me through the crowd?

To prove your valor,
was there really any need of
a crown of thorns for me?"

From childlike faith to the discovery of the sordid truth leads the protagonist to doubt, disbelief and, finally, mistrust. This has been the primeval story of the womankind. Then comes a time when she has cultivated resilience to fear. She has learnt to live among 'serpents' and 'scorpions' – for, she thinks that is the only fate ordained for her.

However, this mood also doesn't last for long. The idea, that of the twin Mithun creation, the female half, which is creative and regenerative can live alone takes hold of the poet and although she is tired and bruised, almost half dead with the lifelong skirmishes she has had, she still hopes that in her nihilistic urge for the decimation of self as a separate entity, both can be one again.

"The fragile ground we stand on is stone cold,
and in the darkness, as we unchain each other
from our hurt and remorse,
the lava of centuries oozes from our hearts,
and we float into each other's eyes.

We savor the darkness bestowed upon us..."

That's how it is. In this section, the sequential treatment of episodic mutualism is resolved in favor of 'floating in each other's eyes', separate but avidly longing for each other. But before that final resolve of 'each for the other, though apart', the poet passes through various moods of crisscrossing faith and denial. The reader sways with the moods as they occur in short pieces and goes along, walking step by step with the poet as she gives a voice to her silently eloquent monologues.

"After a long journey
I have found you,

now resting at your threshold,
in this moonlit night,

I'm waiting for you to know
that I'm here,

I have come all the way
not to try your love for me,

I'm here to tell –
I can't afford not to love anymore!"

A time has come when I must dig up various connotations of the word ancient used as an adjective for all the episodes in this tale. It is Ancient Love, Ancient Quest, and Ancient Remorse – all in the past -, and then Being Nothing and Everything which is a conclusion of sorts - placed in the present – as specified by the word being and contrasted with the past as specified by the word ancient. The word refers not to the past in quantum generality such as near past, but to the past in hoary antiquity or, in other words, before the advent of history. Mythology is full of tales of gods and men entwined in marital and non-marital relationships, tales that are told and retold in every age. Eastern mythology, particularly of the Hindus in India could very well apply to the poet's endeavor to look deep inside the coves of human suffering, particularly of the female of homo sapiens in this frame of reference.

I will borrow only one example from the next segment Ancient Remorse, and then would try to resolve the quandary in the light of the last two sections. Here it is.

"Rooted in defilement,
my heart like a pond of
fresh lilies!

In my silences,
I hear the serpents whisper,
in my pure intoxication,

I let the scorpions crawl
right into my heart!

In my fearlessness,
I do not refuse anything,
that you have to offer me
in the name of love and trust,
assurance and appreciation,

neither do I resist my tears
as you unveil,
you have given me the glory of tasting
the sweetest venom of life
that I accept,

challenging my every impending death,
promising a new life every time
with my last breath."

A pure pond of fresh lilies in which were introduced whispering serpents and crawling scorpions, but even that situation is acceptable because the poet has learnt to partake of the sweetest venom of life. One is reminded of the Hindu mythological story of the Sagar Manthan (the churning of the seas) by gods and demons and the discovery of poison that was consumed by the gods to rid the world of evil. There is no evil here, only death-in-life and life-in-death, a constant struggle between the end and beginning anew; 'impending death' and 'new life' alternating in equal sequential measure. I would call it, not remorse, but resolve when the poet says: promising new life every time / with my last breath.

In fact, nothing ends; new life ensues with every last breath – and the cosmic story of Mithun goes on. 'Being', 'is-ness', 'non-being', 'nothing' – these are mere words, but in terms of Indian meta-mythic frame of reference, these are two sides of the same coin. Nothing is destroyed; it is reborn and then dies again to be reborn again. In this section, the poet ponders over the question with 'ifs' and 'buts', and then finally reaches a conclusion. Drawing from easy to understand constituents of life as we know it, Panch Tattva (air, water, fire, earth, sky), she finally arrives at the much debated answer.

If I'm fire
I must ignite.

If I'm wind
I must blow in a direction my heart indicates.

If I'm rain,
I must pour out to quench thirst of millions like me.

If I'm sky,
I must stretch my wings and fly.

To be Nothing, I must be "All"
and to be All, I must be "Nothing" at last...!

Resolution comes after a long debate, but it does assuredly come. The last part 'Conversations with a friend' is a resolve to see it through. The Mithun union is depicted beautifully in the last lines...

"What difference does it make,
whether you can look into my eyes or not,
when I'm sunken into your pores like the daylight,

and the earth you lie in self-defeat,
despite all your valor,
borrows my heart to throb inside you?"

At the cost of repeating myself, I must say it again with renewed vigor that Kalpna's poetry is a saga of struggle – between the two parts of the dual principle of male-female creation as one. It is the first ever attempt in English to understand, debate and resolve this issue in poetry.

Satyapal Anand

Award winning Poet, Critic and Author of over forty books in Urdu, English, Hindi and Punjabi.

Also by Kalpna Singh-Chitnis

Touched by the Devil
(Poetry Album)

Chand Ka Paivand
(Patch of Moon)

Tafteesh Jari Hai
(The Investigation Continues)

Nishant
(The Dawn)

www.kalpnasinghchitnis.com

BIO

Kalpna Singh-Chitnis is an Indo-American poet, writer, filmmaker and actor based in California, USA. Author of *"Bare Soul"* and three collections of poems in Hindi, she won the prestigious *"Bihar Rajbhasha Award"* (1986-87) given by the government of Bihar, India, for her first poetry collection *"Chand Ka Paivand"* (*Patch of Moon*) before she was 21, and was given the title of *"Bihar Shri"'*(*Jewel of Bihar*) in 1988. She also received the*"Rajiv Gandhi Global Excellence Award"* in 2014 for her contributions to literature and cinema, and was nominated for*"Honor Of Yeast Litteraire"* by *"Levure Litterarie"* magazine. Kalpna's literary works have been widely published in the Indian subcontinent, Europe and North America. She is also the creator and editor of *"Life and Legends"* literary journal, and serves on the Editorial Board of *"Levure litteraire"* in Paris, France.

Kalpna received masters degree in Political Science from *Magadh University, Bodhgaya*, and studied film directing at the *New York Film Academy, Universal Studios,* in *Hollywood.*

She also taught *International Relations* to the postgraduate students at Gaya College, before turning to film directing.

Kalpna's poetry collections *"Tafteesh Jari Hai" (The Investigation Continues)* and *"Nishant" (The Dawn)* have received praise from eminent writers, scholars and critics such as Nobel Prize nominee Dr. Wazir Agha, Naseer Ahmad Nasir, *Vaptsarov Award and Ordre des Arts et des Lettres* winner Amrita Pritam, *Academy Award* winning lyricist, poet and filmmaker Gulzar and others. Kalpna's literary works have been widely published in the Indian subcontinent, Europe and North America, including her translated works of poet Kerdarnath Singh, David Mason, Vishwanath Prasad Tiwari, Christopher Merrill, Naseer Ahmed Nasir, Jennifer Reeser and others. She is the founder and director of the *"Silent River Film and Literary Society"*, and the creator and editor of *"Life and Legends"* literary journal. Known for her feature film *"Goodbye My Friend"* and her short film *"Girl With An Accent"*, Kalpna Singh-Chitnis pioneers in bringing socially conscious cinema to the international platform of the *"Silent River Film Festival"* every year, and promoting Cultural Diplomacy in the East and West. More about Kalpna Singh-Chitnis at *www.kalpnasinghchitnis.com.*